Juniper
Gets
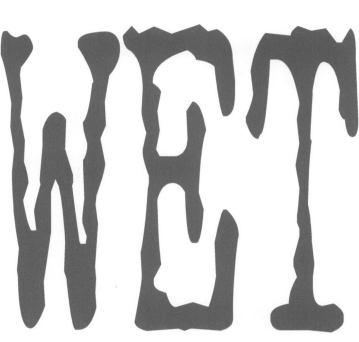

Story by **Bart King**   Illustrated by **Jacob Wenzka**

It had been raining for weeks.

Maybe months.

Maybe even years.

The books had all
been read

and re-read.

The games had all
been played

and played again.

The forts had been built

and abandoned.

Juniper's brothers and sisters were done.
Their imaginations had been spent completely.
All they could do was watch the rain
falling steadily from the gray, gray sky.

But not Juniper. "I'm going outside," she said.

"What are you gonna do?" Joey mumbled.

"You'll get all wet," Allie whined.

Juniper ignored them.

She put on her rain boots,

walked out
the front door,

and opened
her umbrella.

But she didn't
use it.

Instead, she looked up and watched hundreds and thousands of raindrops falling all around her.

Soon, she was completely soaked. But it felt good.

Next, she gathered rocks, lots of rocks,
and put them in the water running through
the gutter at the edge of her street.

The water soon backed into a puddle, and the puddle
spread into a pond, and the pond grew into a lake.

Then she went into the woods to build a boat.

When the water rose to the top of the tallest trees,
Juniper hoisted the canvas and sailed away.

She sailed through small towns

and between the tallest buildings in the biggest cities.

But when water was all she could see
        in every direction, the wind fell away,

and she was stuck.

Fortunately, she had brought along some snacks.

Birds love crackers with peanut butter,
and soon Juniper had lots of new friends.

After everyone had eaten a share,

the birds were happy to help her on her way.

Soon Juniper landed on a tropical island.

She waved goodbye to the birds, gathered her
things, and set off on a long, rugged hike.

She trekked through a lush jungle,

crossed a swiftly
flowing river,

and traversed a high ridge
to reach a beautiful mountaintop castle.

When Juniper arrived, the princess
greeted her in grand fashion.

"Welcome, you are the first visitor
we've had in many years."

Juniper offered her a lollipop from her backpack,

and they became
   great friends.

The princess let Juniper choose a special
gift from the castle's Room of Wonders.

When she finally returned to her boat, the moon was
coming up. But Juniper wasn't tired.

She tucked the gift into her pocket, set course
by the stars, and sailed through the night.

As the sun came up, she saw that
her journey was almost over.

She dove down beneath the boat, through the trees,

and past the window, where she could see her brothers
and sisters still slouched in front of the television.

They perked up when she splashed into the room
and pulled the gift from her wet pocket.

"Where'd ya get that?" they all asked.

"C'mon," Juniper said, "I'll show you!"

"Prepare the submarine for descent,"

Juniper ordered her new crew.

"Aye Aye, Captain!" they all shouted.

And they were on their way.

That night before crawling into her warm, dry bed,
Juniper placed the tiny, plastic gift on her dresser.

As she listened to the rain falling on the roof and the sound of her brothers and sisters sleeping, she wondered what adventures they would dream up next.

The End

for Lucille and Clarice

Thank You to everyone who helped make this project happen!

Aiden & Iley Monroe
All the 5HG kids!
Amelia McGaha
Amelie & Harper
Amelie Moneyhun & Townes Huff
Amos Podvin
Anderson & Knox Hawkins
Anna Freeman
Anna Rodriguez
Armando Huerta & Jeremy Green
Asher Emerson Kovacs
Ava & Ellie McCain
Avery Hannah
Bailey & Brighid
Brendan & Patrick Howe
Caden Alexander
Carol McBroom Smith
Charlie, Brooke, Sydney & Sawyer Roberts
Clarissa & Justin Esguerra-Loy
Cyndie Van Hook
Don & Diane, Matthew & Steven Hereth
Dylan & Fiona Christopherson
Ember Jean
Ethan & Cooper Reynolds
Farrell & Hudson
Flora & Lyla Maldonado Wells
Gaga Jane & Grandpa Wayne
Graham Mansell
GramI & PopL King
Greyson Siefken
Greyson Taubitz
Griffin & Lincoln Masak
Hamilton Hudson
Hampton Heights Pool
Harper & Caleb

Helene Halstead
Hollyn Nation
Howard Luke Anderson
Henry Nicholas McAuley
Linda and Randy Brown
Irene & Perry Luckett
Isabelle & Desmond
J. J. Jackson
J.R.
Jackson & Bailey Neely
Jennifer & Arpit
Jess Jensen-Ryan
Joe Morgan
Joe Willey
John & Samantha
Joshua Green & Anna Bengel
Juniper & Vivian Wagoner
Justin Moss
Kammy Kupkake
Keiyo Pridgen
Larry, Marenn & Katelynn Morrison
Laura & Michael Cape
Laurel Bleich
Lauren McGuire
Lazlo, Eike, & Levin
Lilith & Alexis Rose
Lisa Carpenter
Liz Bowen
Logan & Gabriella Devine-McWilliams
Lucie Claire & Hawkes Corbett
M + M
Maggie McEnerny
Maria, Clyde, Roscoe & Jonah
Mavis Nichol
Miles Silas

Nancy & Don Walton
Nate L
Noe & Q
Papa Larry & Sissie Wright
Patrick Armstrong
Peg Wenzka
pOp Grampzka
Rainey Lynch
Ralph & Sheri Brown
Reagan & Cane Wilbur
Roddy & Hayes Boatwright
Sadie, Adrian & Tyler
Sandy Reichert
Savannah & Luke Buchanan
Sophie, Faye & Abe Block
Stacey Morris
Susan (Suess)
Susan Gantzer
The Anderson Family
The Glude Family
The Little Children
The Przystawik Family
The Rambus Family
The Reed Family
The Schwartz Family
The Thurston Family
The Tooleys
The Walton & Seuser children
The Yabsley-Hernandez family
Tracy "Big T" Baker
Tucker & Amelia Arnett
Valentine Wolfe
Victor, Ian & Sylvia Feldman
Vincent & Hansie Vaden
Will & Maya Brown
Wilma
Zachary Bastin

Juniper Gets Wet is the creation of two dads who met around a kiddie pool in Athens, Georgia, during the rainy summer of 2013.

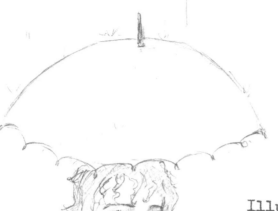

Illustrator: Jacob Wenzka

Jacob Wenzka is a father of two, with a Batchelor's Degree of Fine Art from UGA. He has been painting for nearly two decades, and has recently begun working as an illustrator. This is the second complete book, and his first book for children.

Author: Bart King

Bart King is a father, writer, musician and communications consultant. He also is the co-founder of BossParent.com, a resource for parents to learn about child behavior and development to improve family life.

Order copies of Juniper Gets Wet at BossParent.com/Juniper